I0411567

United States
Department of
Agriculture

Forest Service

Pacific Southwest
Research Station

Research Paper
PSW-RP-257
June 2008

The Experience of Community Residents in a Fire-Prone Ecosystem: A Case Study on the San Bernardino National Forest

George T. Cvetkovich and Patricia L. Winter

The Forest Service of the U.S. Department of Agriculture is dedicated to the principle of multiple use management of the Nation's forest resources for sustained yields of wood, water, forage, wildlife, and recreation. Through forestry research, cooperation with the States and private forest owners, and management of the National Forests and National Grasslands, it strives—as directed by Congress—to provide increasingly greater service to a growing Nation.

Authors

George T. Cvetkovich is professor of psychology and Interim Director, Center for Cross-Cultural Research, Western Washington University, Department of Psychology, 516 High Street, Bellingham, WA 98225-9089; e-mail: cvet@wwu.edu. **Patricia L. Winter** is a research social scientist, U.S. Department of Agriculture, Forest Service, Pacific Southwest Research Station, Wildland Recreation and Urban Cultures Research Unit, 4955 Canyon Crest Drive, Riverside, CA 92507-6099; e-mail: pwinter@fs.fed.us.

Cover
Lower right photo courtesy of RIMOFTHEWORLD.net.

Abstract

Cvetkovich, George T.; Winter, Patricia L. 2008. The experience of community residents in a fire-prone ecosystem: a case study on the San Bernardino National Forest. Res. Pap. PSW-RP-257. Albany, CA: U.S. Department of Agriculture, Forest Service, Pacific Southwest Research Station. 42 p.

This report presents results from a study of San Bernardino National Forest community residents' experiences with and perceptions of fire, fire management, and the Forest Service. Using self-administered surveys and focus group discussions, we found that participants had personal experiences with fire, were concerned about fire, and felt knowledgeable about effective fire management. Consideration of future consequences, a measure of time orientation, was not found to be related to beliefs about and reactions to wildfire. Trust in the Forest Service was related to a number of fire-associated attitudes. Findings help shed light on the experiences of residents living in fire-prone communities and highlight the importance of trust in understanding public perceptions about fire management.

Key words: Fire-prone communities, San Bernardino National Forest, fire management, trust, salient values similarity.

Summary

Residents of fire-prone communities proximate to and surrounded by the San Bernardino National Forest participated in this study. As a group, the participants are characterized as having personally experienced wildland-fire-related events, being highly concerned about fires and fire risks, and self-assessed as knowledgeable about what effective fire management should be. This report presents results of completed questionnaires and focus group comments organized around reactions to and beliefs about wildfires and wildfire management. These are (1) personal stress-related consequences of directly experiencing wildfires and living in communities threatened by wildfires, concern about the risk of wildfires, and assessments of level of knowledge about wildfire management; (2) perceived level of responsibility for wildfire prevention, participation in fire management activities, and perceived barriers to effective fire management; and (3) views about preferred ways of receiving communication and education about wildfires and management. The report also presents analyses of the relationship between these reactions and beliefs and two measures of individual differences. Consideration of future consequences, a measure of individual differences in future time perspective found to be associated with differences in environmental attitudes and behaviors in previous research, was not strongly correlated to wildfire-related reactions and beliefs. High trust of the Forest Service was related to having fewer direct experiences with fire and related stress reactions, giving the Forest Service a high grade for efforts to prevent fires in the past year, and agreeing that the past record of fire management was a good reason to rely on the Forest Service. Participants trusting the Forest Service also agreed that the Forest Service shared their values for wildland fire management, that the Forest Service's management actions had been consistent with shared values, and that any value/action inconsistencies were justified.

Contents

Introduction

Conditions in the national forests resulting from drought, bark beetle infestation, abundant fuel supplies owing to fire suppression, high tree densities, and arson (Molloy 2004) have resulted in a high threat of wildland fire. In 2003, one expert summarized the destruction from wildfires since 1990 as follows:

> [W]e have lost 50 million acres of forest to wildfire and suffered the destruction of over 4,800 homes. The fires of 2000 burned 8.4 million acres and destroyed 861 structures. The 2002 fire season resulted in a loss of 6.9 million acres and 2,381 structures destroyed, including 835 homes. These staggering losses from wildfire also resulted in taxpayers paying $2.9 billion in firefighting costs. This does not include vast sums spent to rehabilitate damaged forests and replace homes [Bonnicksen 2003].

Since then, the San Bernardino National Forest, the focus of this study, has experienced major fires such as the Old Fire in 2003 and the Esperanza Fire in 2006. These and other fires have added to the toll through the burning of hundreds of thousands of additional acres of forest, the destruction of hundreds of homes and other property, the loss of human lives, and a high cost for firefighting (U.S. Department of Agriculture Inspector General 2006). The communities included in this study are adjacent to the national forest and other federal lands and have been listed by the California Department of Forestry and Fire Protection as Hazard Level Code "3," indicating the highest fire threat level (Inland Empire Fire Safe Alliance 2006).

This study examines three broadly grouped sets of reactions to and beliefs about wildfires and wildfire management: (1) personal stress-related consequences of directly experiencing wildland fires and living in communities threatened by wildfires, concern about the risk of wildland fires, and assessments of level of knowledge about wildfire management; (2) perceived level of responsibility for wildfire prevention, participation in fire management activities, and perceived barriers to effective fire management; and (3) views about preferred ways of receiving communication and education about wildfires and management. This information is presented in two parts: (1) results relating to reactions and beliefs about wildfires and (2) relationship of the reactions and beliefs to two factors–consideration of future consequences and trust of the USDA Forest Service (and associated measures).

Consideration of Future Consequences

Consideration of future consequences is a form of future time perspective that motivates an individual's efforts to reach desirable outcomes by focusing either on distant or immediate consequences of potential behaviors (Strathman et al.

1994). A reliable and valid measure of consideration of future consequences has been developed and was used in this study (Joireman 1999, Joireman et al. 2004, Petrocelli 2003). Individual differences in level of consideration of future consequences have been found to be related to various health and environment-related attitudes and behaviors. These include attitudes concerning private automobiles versus public transportation (Collins and Chambers 2005; Joireman et al. 2001, 2004), recycling and waste reduction (Ebreo and Vining 2001), sensitivity to health communications (Orbell et at. 2004), and intentions to perform health behaviors (Sirois 2004).

The general question addressed by this study is, how do those who give more consideration to long-term consequences differ from those who give more consideration to short-term consequences with regard to reactions and beliefs about wildfires and management? Are those who give more consideration to long-term consequences more likely to be concerned about wildfires, for example? Are they more likely to engage in risk reduction activities (such as taking defensible space measures around their homes)? Do they have particular preferences concerning how they receive information about wildfires?

Salient Value Similarity and Trust of the USDA Forest Service

Trust, the psychological willingness to rely on others or cooperate because of positive expectations of another person's intentions or behavior (Rousseau et al. 1998), is an important component of public responses to a broad range of risks (Siegrist 2000, Siegrist et al. 2000). Trust seems to be issue and situation specific (Kneeshaw et al. 2004, Langer 2002, Winter et al. 2004). An agency might be more trusted to manage one particular risk than another risk. Trust has been documented as an essential component of effective communication surrounding risk management (Covello et al. 1986, Freudenberg and Rursch 1994, Johnson 2004, Slovic 2000). Those who trust the source of a communication are more likely to believe the communicated message and more likely to accept initiatives designed to address that risk, including actions they must take themselves. In addition, trust has been found to be an important component of public responses to wildfire management (e.g., Liljeblad and Borrie 2006; Shindler et al. 2004; Winter et al. 2004; Winter and Cvetkovich 2004a, 2004b).

Among studies examining trust related to forest-management issues, those most closely related to this study examined the interactions between salient values similarity and trust. In these studies, salient values similarity was a significant predictor of public trust in the Forest Service to address a number of natural resource management issues including a proposed program of research (Cvetkovich et al.

Those who trust the source of a communication are more likely to believe the communicated message and more likely to accept initiatives designed to address that risk.

1995), a recreation fee demonstration program (Winter et al. 1999), and acceptance of approaches to manage threatened and endangered species (Cvetkovich and Winter 1998, 2003; Winter and Knap 2001). Other significant influences that have been explored in studies of trust related to forest-management issues include community of interest and place, ethnicity, gender, concern about the management issue in question, and knowledge about the target topic (Winter and Cvetkovich 2007).

In one study (Cvetkovich and Winter 2003), participants repeatedly raised the issues of the perceived consistency between Forest Service actions and similar salient values. From this we built a pair of items and tested them with publics regarding issues of endangered species management (Cvetkovich and Winter 2003) and fire management (Cvetkovich and Winter 2007). Perceived consistency between similar salient values and Forest Service actions, and justification of perceived inconsistency were instrumental in further understanding patterns of trust and distrust among publics. These findings are outlined in greater detail elsewhere (Cvetkovich and Winter 2004). The previous study of attitudes toward fire and fire management (Cvetkovich and Winter 2007) involved random samples of residents residing in four Southwestern States, including those with little direct experience with fire. In this study, we attempted to confirm that consistency and justification of inconsistency contribute to trust of Forest Service fire management, this time among communities known to have direct personal experiences with fire. Some of those receiving results from our four-state study asked us to report on residents' views that were known to be directly affected by fire risk. This study addresses their request.

Methods

Participants

Residents and homeowners (n = 89) in fire-prone communities surrounded by the San Bernardino National Forest[1] participated in this study (table 1). We sought to obtain a purposive sample, rather than a random sample, of selected community areas, using key-contact and snowball approaches linked to the preexisting groups. Participants were invited through fire safe councils, local announcements in newspapers and radio stations, an e-mail tree through a forest district focusing on partnerships, and personal phone calls from the investigators. The majority (57.3 percent) of participants were male, White (92.1 percent), 55 years of age or older (68.6 percent), with at least some college education (85.3 percent, with 30.3 percent reporting some graduate study). A little more than one-fourth of participants (25.8 percent) had total household incomes

---

[1] One community is located in a part of the San Bernardino National Forest managed by the Angeles National Forest.

Table 1—Schedule of focus groups and number of participants

Date	Location	Number of participants
March 18th	Angelus Oaks	12
March 21st	Forest Falls	8
March 22nd	Lake Arrowhead	3
March 23rd	Crestline	14
March 25th	Big Bear	7
March 26th	Wrightwood	12
March 30th	Idyllwild	17
March 31st	Lake Arrowhead	9
April 1st	Crestline	4
April 1st	Forest Falls	3

of $49,999 or less. Other participants reported incomes from $50,000 to $74,999 (13.5 percent), or $75,000 or greater (42.7 percent).

A note on participation—

Some community residents did not participate because of road closures or weather-related concerns (we had an unusual series of snowstorms, icy roads, and fog during the study period that came late in the season and kept many away because of safety concerns). A few residents expressed the feeling of being "meetinged out," considering what they judged to be an extensive number of meetings related to fire issues within their communities. Some told us they would only attend if a direct tangible benefit from their participation could be identified in advance of the meeting, while others expressed the feeling that they were waiting for action on prior meetings already held about fire management issues of concern to them before they would participate in more. Others told us they felt there was not adequate notice about our meetings. This was in spite of the radio and newspaper announcements, including media Web sites, as well as e-mail notices and telephone calls from the researchers or through fire safe councils. Identifying the most effective communication networks, including those that are community based, was an important part of our research effort, and we had only partial success. On one forest district, many of our contacts came through an e-mail tree derived from various partnership and collaborative efforts. This proved an invaluable resource to us, and the direct contact from someone residents knew in the Forest Service helped pave the way. We found that a number of routes and contacts were necessary. These routes differed greatly and in some ways reflected the unique nature of the communities we tried to reach.

Survey Instrument

A self-administered questionnaire (app. A) created for this study included a number of Likert-type items focusing on three sets of reactions to and beliefs about wildfires and wildfire management:

1. Personal stress-related consequences of directly experiencing wildfires and living in communities threatened by wildfires (a series of yes/no items, adapted from the Impact of Event Scale-Revised, cited in Weiss and Marmar 1996) concern about the risk of wildfires (concern held by self and judged concern of other residents), and assessments of level of knowledge about wildfire management (self, residents, and Forest Service).

2. The perceived level of responsibility for wildfire prevention of various parties, effectiveness of risk reduction among responsible parties, personal participation in fire management activities (a series of yes/no items), and perceived barriers to effective fire management.

3. Views about preferred ways of receiving communication and education about wildfires and management.

In addition, a 12-item measure of consideration of future consequences created by Strathman et al. (1994) was included on the questionnaire. Measures of trust, salient values similarity, value consistency of actions, and justification of inconsistencies were adapted from earlier research reviewed in Cvetkovich and Winter (2007).

Focus Group Protocol

Participants were led through a series of discussion topics regarding fire and fire management on the San Bernardino National Forest (app. B). These items included objectives for fire management, concerns in fire management, alternatives to accomplish fire management objectives, shared values and trust in Forest Service fire management, and preferences for receiving communication and education.

Procedure

Each session lasted approximately 1½ hours and started with a statement of purpose of the study, the voluntary nature of responses, importance of respect of other views in the discussion, and ability to opt out of any questions that made the participant uncomfortable. Participants completed the self-administered questionnaire and then were led through the discussion topics. Each discussion was audio taped; a

Participants completed the self-administered questionnaire and then were led through the discussion topics.

notetaker recorded key comments and concepts to help anchor the transcription of audio records. Notes and surveys were matched through assigned identification numbers, allowing comparison between written and verbal responses.[2] Ten sessions were conducted over a 3-week period.

Results

Reactions and Beliefs About Wildfires and Management

Personal experiences with fire—

Participants reported a number of personal experiences with fire during their lifetimes. The vast majority had encountered wildland-fire related events such as seeing a fire (96.6 percent), smelling smoke (89.9 percent), and experiencing road closure (87.6 percent). Additional experiences shared by the majority included evacuation from their homes (69.7 percent), having power shut off to reduce fire risk (65.2 percent), and having a prescribed burn near their homes (62.9 percent). Less common were loss or damage to personal property of family, friend, or close neighbor (44.9 percent); personal loss or damage to property (15.7 percent); health problems or discomfort (15.7 percent); personal injury (5.6 percent); and family, friend, or neighbor suffering injuries (5.6 percent). Reported health problems were

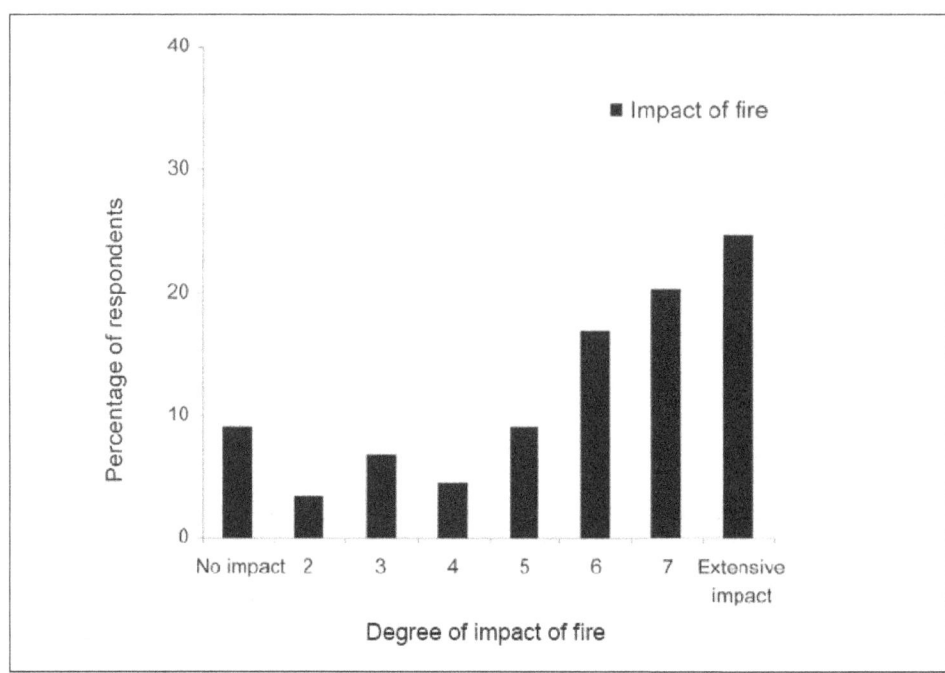

Figure 1—Degree of impact that fire on the San Bernardino National Forest has had on respondents.

---

[2] Participation was completely anonymous. Although first names and brief introductions were shared for group facilitation purposes, these were not recorded and only participant identification numbers were used in the gathering and recording of data. Participants were informed in advance that their responses and comments would be handled in this manner, in order to facilitate openness and candor.

primarily smoke-related. On average, 6 of the 11 personal experiences listed were reported by each respondent. In judging the direct, personal impact of fire, a majority of participants (61.8 percent) selected a 6, 7, or 8 on the 8-point impact scale (1 = no impact, 8 = extensive impact) with only about one-tenth (9 percent) selecting 1, "no impact." In sum, the vast majority had personally experienced a number of fire-related impacts, and fire was judged to have a direct personal impact on most of the respondents' lives (fig. 1).

Personal consequences of fire and fire risk—
The impact of living in a fire-prone ecosystem was examined through stress-related effects. Almost one-third of participants had not experienced any of the 21 listed possible difficulties resulting from wildland fire risk (the modal response was 1) in the past 7 days. Those reporting a greater number of fire-related experiences rated themselves as having more fire-related difficulties (as defined by the Weiss and Marmar scale, $r = 0.37$, $p < 0.001$, $n = 83$). Slightly more than one-third (38.2 percent) agreed that "I avoided letting myself get upset when I thought about it or was reminded of it," and almost one-third (29.2 percent) reported "any reminder brought back feelings about it," as well as "I felt watchful or on guard." About one-fourth (25.8 percent) reported that "other things kept making me think about it," and that "pictures about it popped into my mind" (24.7 percent). About one-fifth (18.0 percent) thought about it when they didn't mean to. Approximately one-tenth of our respondents reported "I had waves of strong feelings about it" (13.5 percent), "I tried not to think about it" (11.2 percent), "I felt irritable and angry" (9.0 percent), and feeling like they were back in a time when there was no fire (9.0 percent). Reporting of physical symptoms (sweating, trouble breathing, or nausea) was rare (only 3.4 percent). However, more than one-third (41.0 percent) indicated that more than one difficulty was experienced within the past 7 days. These results do not indicate major disruptions to everyday functioning. They do suggest that there is a continuing psychological impact from fire and fire risk even a few years after the last major fire in the local area.

> **There is a continuing psychological impact from fire and fire risk even a few years after the last major fire in the local area.**

Concern about fire risk and knowledge about fire management—
Participants rated their personal concern about fires and fire risks as high ($M = 7.43$, SD = 0.99; 1 = not at all concerned, 8 = very concerned; fig. 2). Other community residents were also perceived as concerned, but not as concerned as self ($M = 6.70$, SD = 1.38; $F_{(1, 85)} = 23.08$, $p < 0.01$; fig. 2).

Personal knowledge of what effective fire management should be done was rated as high ($M = 6.13$, SD = 1.60; 1 = not very knowledgeable, 8 = very knowledgeable; fig. 3), but lower than ratings assigned to knowledge of fire management

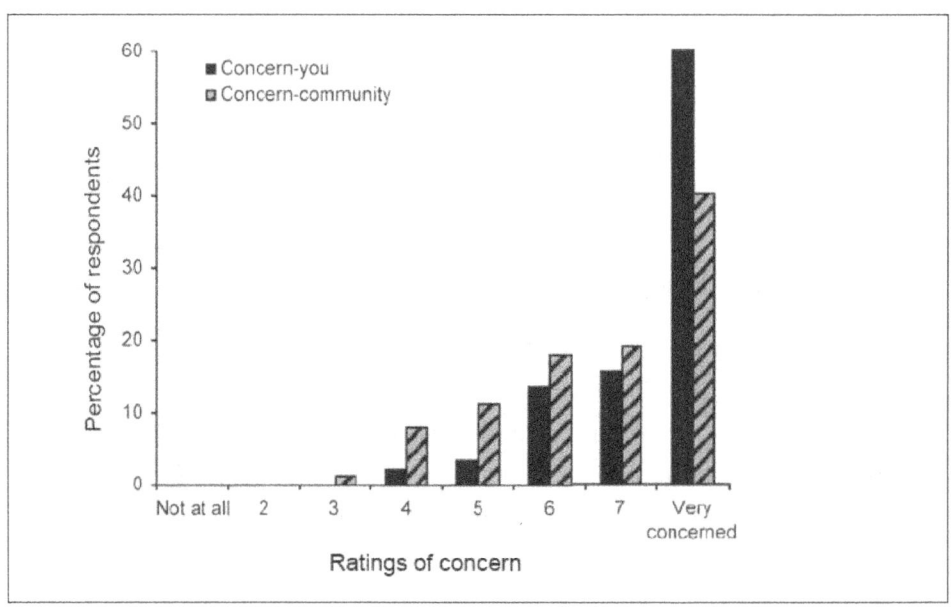

Figure 2—Ratings of concern of self and other community residents on the San Bernardino National Forest.

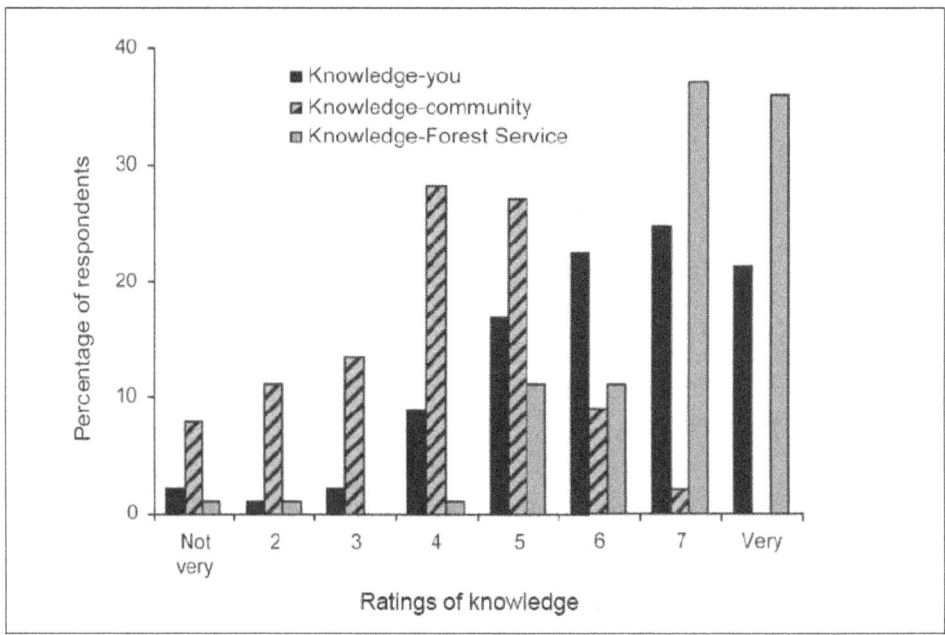

Figure 3—Ratings of knowledge of each party about what should be done for effective fire management on the San Bernardino National Forest.

held by the Forest Service ($M = 6.86$, SD = 1.32; $F_{(1, 85)} = 13.70$, $p < 0.001$, fig. 3). The knowledge of other community residents ($M = 3.92$, SD = 1.48; fig. 3) was rated as lower than both the level of one's own knowledge ($F_{(1, 85)} = 139.71$, $p < 0.001$) and that of the Forest Service ($F_{(1, 85)} = 287.45$, $p < 0.001$).

Participants who rated their own concern and knowledge as high also tended to rate the concern and knowledge of other community members as high ($r = 0.31$,

$p < 0.004$, n = 86 and r = 0.36, $p = 0.001$, n = 88, respectively). Judgments of Forest Service knowledge were not related to judgment of own knowledge (r = 0.19, $p = 0.08$, n = 88), but those who rated the knowledge of other citizens as high also rated the Forest Service's level of knowledge as high (r = 0.32, $p = 0.02$, n = 88). In sum, participants characterized their own concern and knowledge as higher than but similar to that of other community members, particularly if other community members shared their values. The Forest Service was characterized as more knowledgeable than either self or other community members.

Perceived Responsibility for Fire Management

Perceived responsibility for fire management was assessed by asking participants to distribute 100 points among 10 potentially responsible parties. An "other" option was provided so that respondents could add parties to the list. Respondents could leave point assignments blank or enter "0" for no responsibility for reduction of fire risk. A followup question asked respondents to assign a grade to any party they had assigned points to. The grade was based on how well in the past 12 months the party had reduced the risk of wildland fires on the San Bernardino Mountains.

As shown in table 2, of the listed parties, the Forest Service was judged by the largest number of participants (over 80 percent) to have at least some responsibility

Table 2—Number of points (out of 100) of responsibility in reducing the risk of wildland fires and grade on how well each party has done in the past 12 months in reducing the risk of wildland fires on the San Bernardino Mountains

	Participants assigning 1 or more points	Median responsibility	Mean responsibility	Std. Dev.	Range of points	Median grade
	Percent					
USDA Forest Service	98	20	18.68	11.89	5-80	B
California Department of Forestry	91	10	14.27	10.01	2–50	B
Local fire departments	88	10	11.51	8.32	5–20	A
Me and the people who live with me	88	10	11.81	12.39	1–80	B
My local community	88	10	10.79	9.06	3–50	C
Visitors and tourists	76	5	5.58	6.47	1–30	D
Federal legislators and representatives	75	10	8.79	8.60	1–40	C
State legislators and representatives	70	5	6.70	6.23	1–25	C
Scientists and researchers	61	5	4.21	4.35	1–20	C
Local business owners	61	5	5.00	3.94	1–13	C
Other	9	10	12.73	15.23	5–50	F

and on average (both mean and median) was assigned the largest responsibility, around 20 points. Ratings of responsibility suggest that after the Forest Service, the California Department of Forestry (now called Cal Fire) is viewed as having a primary responsibility. It is also interesting that "me and the people who live with me" received fairly high responsibility ratings.

The Forest Service received a median grade of B for its fire-reduction efforts over the last year. Six of the listed parties were assigned a median responsibility of around 10 percent. One of these, "my local fire department," was assigned a grade of A. The California Department of Forestry and "me and the people who live with me," received grades of B. The remaining two, "my local community" and "federal legislators and representatives," received a grade of C.

Only nine participants identified a responsible "other" in addition to those listed. Identified "others" included "lawsuits and regulations," "local/county planning and regulations," "environmental groups," and "fire safe councils." These self-identified parties were assessed as having relatively high responsibility of around 10 points. Opting to identify a party not listed seemed to be prompted by a desire to identify those perceived as not doing a good job. Eight of the nine reported "others" were graded as deserving either a D or an F.

The remaining four listed parties were assigned an average of five points of responsibility. Three of these received an average grade of C. The fourth, "Visitors and tourists," received a grade of D.

Goals of Fire Management

During the focus group, discussion participants were asked, "What objectives for fire management are critical for this forest? Specifically, what should fire management accomplish on this forest...what should it do?" Several of the 143 responses identified the major goal of fire management to be the reduction of tree density (18.2 percent of responses), fuel removal (7.7 percent), and/or prescribed burns (3.5 percent) in order to establish and maintain a healthy "natural" forest (10.5 percent). Some concern was expressed about both the risks of prescribed burns and the need for communicating to residents when they were occurring (2.8 percent) and having the protection of people and property as the major goal of fire management (2.8 percent). Education about wildland fire and management was also expressed as an important goal (9.1 percent). Some participants were particularly concerned that not enough was being done focused on communicating to and educating nonresident tourists and backcountry users (2.1 percent). Appropriately timed closures of high risk areas were also identified as a technique for reaching fire management goals (2.1 percent). The planning and control of residential and other human development was also identified as an important component of effective fire management (5.6 percent). Three aspects of management during fire events were mentioned. These were the need for communication between officials and the public (5.6 percent), getting up-to-date news about the status of evacuation routes (5.6 percent), and coordination between different agencies (3.5 percent).

Fire Management Activities

A number of actions that could effectively reduce fire risk were reported. Most people had read about what could be done to protect their homes from wildland fires (97.8 percent), had implemented defensible space around their property (94.4 percent), and had attended a public meeting about wildland fire (93.3 percent).[3] A majority had also reduced flammable vegetation on their property because they were required to do it (75.3 percent), worked with a community effort focused on fire protection (75.3 percent), made inquiries of the local fire safe council or volunteers on how to reduce fire risk (73.0 percent), made inquires of the local fire department on how to reduce fire risk (64.0 percent), and made inquiries of the local forest ranger (56.2 percent). A little over a third had changed the structure of their home to reduce risk (38.2 percent) and/or worked on a wildland fire suppression effort either in a paid or volunteer position (38.2 percent). Others had volunteered through various efforts or had worked through a fire safe council. An overall judgment yielded a moderately high evaluation of the effectiveness of these actions ($M = 6.01$, SD = 1.55, n = 85, median = 6; 1 = not at all effective, 8 = extremely effective).

Table 3—Reported barriers to personal fire management activities

Barrier	Checked "yes"
	Percent
Inadequate financial resources	22.6
Own physical limitations	22.6
Don't want to change the landscape	21.8
Don't want to change my roof or other built structures	20.7
Not worried about fire risk	19.8
Not sure what will work	14.3
Don't know who to call/hire	3.6

> **Most people had read about what could be done to protect their homes from wildland fires, had implemented defensible space around their property, and had attended a public meeting about wildland fire.**

---

[3] We expect this high number is characteristic of the intensive effort to reduce fire risk and to raise awareness of fire management efforts in the participating communities.

Barriers to Personal Action

From about 4 percent to a little over 20 percent of participants indicated that their own fire reduction effort had been hindered because of one of the listed barriers (table 3). "Inadequate financial resources," "Own physical limitations," and "Don't want to change the landscape" were the most frequently reported barriers, followed closely by "Don't want to change my roof or other built structures" and "Not worried about fire risk." "Not sure what will work," and "Don't know who to call/hire" were the least frequently reported barriers.

Participants with lower incomes were more likely than those with higher incomes to report the barriers of "Own physical limitations" ($r = -0.41$, $p < 0.001$, n = 71), "Not sure what will work" ($r = -0.35$, $p < 0.001$, n = 85), "Not worried" ($r = -0.29$, $p < 0.02$, n = 71), "Inadequate financial resources" ($r = -0.27$, $p < 0.03$, n = 70), and "Don't want to change the landscape" ($r = -0.24$, $p < 0.05$, n = 72). Gender, age, and education level were not correlated with reported barriers.

Barriers to Others' Actions

A sizable number of participants concluded that effective reduction of fire risk has been hindered because at least one of the other involved parties had not done its part. About one-half (50.6 percent) believe that their neighbors have not done their part; about one-third (29.2 percent) believe public agencies have not done their part; and about one-fifth (22.5 percent) believe the Forest Service has not done its part. Those who reported that their neighbors have not done their part were also likely to cite the inactivity of public agencies ($r = 0.47$, $p < 0.001$, n = 85) and the Forest Service ($r = 0.36$, $p < 0.001$, n = 82) as barriers to reducing fire risk. Other barriers to effective risk reduction added by respondents in an open-ended question identified land use policies, growth and housing, community restrictions on removal of trees and vegetation, a lack of coordination between agencies, and environmentalists.

Communication and Education

Participants had many views on approaches to communication, collaboration, and education about fire management. The most preferred sources of information were public meetings the Forest Service leads so the community can ask questions (88.8 percent) and community meetings (84.3 percent). Other information sources preferred included a Web site (79.8 percent), brochures and pamphlets available on request (77.5 percent), articles in the local paper (77.5 percent), an e-mail tree sent by Forest Service representative and forwarded by fire safe council volunteers (75.3 percent), local television/radio spots put on by local Forest Service ranger (64.0

The most preferred sources of information were public meetings the Forest Service leads so the community can ask questions, and community meetings.

percent), and information and displays at Forest Service visitor center (60.7 percent). Additional suggestions included e-mails directly from the Forest Service, signs, a hotline or number residents could call to speak directly with someone knowledgeable, and messages on community bulletin boards. Flyers and newsletters left on residence doors were also brought up as a means of "getting the word out." It should be noted that the strong support for community meetings and direct engagement with the Forest Service was expressed by participants who themselves had come to participate in a meeting. As noted earlier, some residents expressed clear hesitation to participate in yet another meeting about fire.

Consideration of Future Consequences

The 12-item consideration of future consequences (CFC) scale (table 4) used to examine future orientation among respondents showed a comparatively high future orientation (alpha = 0.522).

The average CFC score for participants (M = 4.15, SD = 0.50, n = 89) was slightly higher (suggesting participants are somewhat more oriented to the future) than that reported in earlier research on college students (Petrocelli 2003). The vast majority (94.4 percent) had a score of either 4 or 5 (CFC was either "somewhat" or "extremely" characteristic). A higher CFC score was correlated to being more educated (r = 0.39, n = 89, p < 0.01) but not to gender (r = 0.15, n = 89, p > 0.05), age (r = -0.05, n = 88, p > -0.05), years living in current home (r = -0.08, n = 87, p > 0.05), or years living in the San Bernardino National Forest (r = -0.04, n = 88, p > 0.05).

Consideration of future consequences scores were correlated to only a few measures of reactions to and beliefs about wildfires and wildfire management. Participants who indicated that they gave more consideration to future consequences more often reported that they had inquired at their local fire department about how to reduce fire risk (r = 0.23, p < 0.05, n = 87). They were also likely to report that they found themselves acting or feeling as though they were back in a time where there was a fire (r = 0.30, p < 0.01, n = 82), although they were less likely to feel irritable or angry (r = - 0.23, p < 0.05, n = 83).

Trust, Salient Values, and Reasons for Relying on the Forest Service

Participants' ratings of the salient values similarity items indicated a perception of shared values ("shares values": M = 6.61, SD = 1.53, median = 7, n = 85; "similar goals": M = 6.37, SD = 1.75, median = 7, n = 84; "supports views": M = 6.31, SD = 1.56, median = 6, n = 81). Less than 5 percent of the participants provided ratings below the midrange on each of these items, indicating dissimilar values. Of the 44 comments made during the focus group discussions concerning the values shared

Table 4—Responses to the consideration of future consequences (CFC) scale

CFC item	Extremely uncharacteristic	Somewhat uncharacteristic	Uncertain	Somewhat characteristic	Extremely characteristic	Don't know
I consider how things might be in the future, and try to influence those things with my day to day behavior.	0	2.2	2.2	48.3	47.2	0
Often I engage in a particular behavior in order to achieve outcomes that may not result for many years.	6.7	2.2	16.9	29.2	40.4	2.2
I only act to satisfy immediate concerns, figuring the future will take care of itself.	58.4	23.6	4.5	4.5	0	9.0
My behavior is only influenced by the immediate (i.e., a matter of days or weeks) outcomes of my actions.	56.2	19.1	6.7	5.6	1.1	10.1
My convenience is a big factor in the decisions I make or the actions I take.	30.3	25.8	18.0	19.1	2.2	3.4
I am willing to sacrifice my immediate happiness or well-being in order to achieve future outcomes.	4.5	9.0	7.9	55.1	23.6	0
I think it is important to take warnings about negative outcomes seriously even if the negative outcome will not occur for many years.	1.1	2.2	6.7	41.6	47.2	1.1
I think it is more important to perform a behavior with important distant consequences than a behavior with less-important immediate consequences.	1.1	4.5	24.7	39.3	28.1	1.1
I generally ignore warnings about possible future problems because I think the problems will be resolved before they reach a crisis level.	58.4	18.0	9.0	6.7	2.2	4.5
I think that sacrificing now is usually unnecessary since future outcomes can be dealt with at a later time.	55.1	23.6	7.9	9.0	1.1	3.4
I only act to satisfy immediate concerns, figuring that I will take care of future problems that may occur at a later date.	59.6	18.0	7.9	6.7	2.2	4.5
Since my day to day work has specific outcomes, it is more important to me than behavior that has distant outcomes.	37.1	32.6	9.0	11.2	5.6	2.2

with the Forest Service, 4.7 percent related to the preservation of life and property and nearly 26 percent (25.6 percent) related to protection of the forest and natural habitat.

Since ratings of "shares values," "same goals," and "supports views" were highly intercorrelated (r = 0.70 to 0.74, $p < 0.001$, n = 81 to 84), a single index of "Salient Value Similarity of the Forest Service" (SVS) was computed based on the mean of responses to these three questions. This scale showed high reliability (alpha = 0.88) and was used in subsequent analyses.

Participants were also asked to what extent they trust the Forest Service in their fire management efforts. Based on an 8-point scale (1 = I completely distrust the Forest Service, 8 = I completely trust the Forest Service), responses leaned towards trust (M = 5.85, SD = 1.68, median = 6, n = 86; fig. 4), with the majority (64 percent) providing ratings of 6 through 8 on the trust item. Trust of the Forest Service was reflected in comments such as: "I think we're on the same page with the Forest Service"; "We are real fortunate, because the Forest Service has been a good partner"; "We love where we live. We love looking at the beautiful mountains and everything up here. They [the Forest Service] want to maintain that and we want to maintain that too"; and "One thing the local Forest Service has in common with the community is to preserve the forest."

As expected based on the salient values similarity model described in the introduction, trust of the Forest Service was significantly correlated to SVS (r = 0.69, $p < 0.001$, n = 81). Participants who believed that the Forest Service shared their values, had the same goals, and supported their views concerning fire protection also trusted the Forest Service's fire management.

Participants who believed that the Forest Service shared their values, had the same goals, and supported their views concerning fire protection also trusted the Forest Service's fire management.

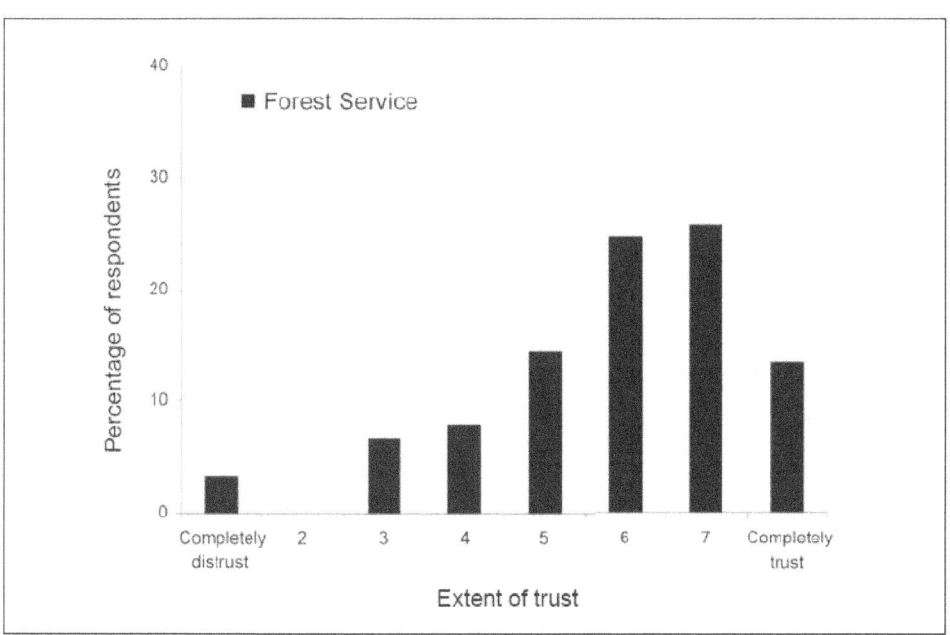

Figure 4—Extent of trust in the fire management efforts of the Forest Service.

When asked the extent to which fellow community residents share their values about fire management, the average response was above the midpoint on the scale, indicating moderately shared values ($M = 5.58$, SD = 1.55, median = 6, n = 81). Participants who perceived that their values were shared by other community residents rated community residents concern about wildfire as high (r = 0.42, $p < 0.001$, n = 80).

Respondents were asked if they thought that people were generally not trustworthy (value of 1) or generally trustworthy (value of 8, with value scale ranging from 1 to 8). Trustworthiness of others was rated fairly high ($M = 6.45$, SD = 1.60, median = 7, n = 88). Those who found others to be trustworthy were also likely to indicate that they trusted the Forest Service (r = 0.49, $p < 0.001$, n = 85).

Reasons for reliance—

Participants indicated whether a series of items were reasons to rely on the Forest Service's fire management on the San Bernardino National Forest. A majority agreed or strongly agreed that the following were good reasons for relying on the Forest Service: "Procedures that ensure the Forest Service uses effective fire management" (67.4 percent), "Personal relationships I have with Forest Service personnel" (59.6 percent), and "The Forest Service's past record of fire management" (58.4 percent). A majority felt that the following were not reasons to rely on the Forest Service: "Media coverage of Forest Service fire management" (60.7 percent said this was not a reason), and "Congress holds the Forest Service accountable for its fire management" (52.8 percent said this was not a reason). Participants were almost equally divided on "Opportunities that I have to voice my views about fire management"; 38.2 percent said this was not a reason, 46.1 percent said it was a reason.

As shown in table 5, compared to those with less trust, those with more trust agreed that good reasons to rely on the Forest Service included "The Forest Service's past record of fire management," "Procedures that ensure the Forest Service uses effective fire management," and "Media coverage of Forest Service fire management." Compared to those who perceived less value similarity with the Forest Service, those who perceived more value similarity agreed that these three were good reasons to rely on the Forest Service as well as "Laws controlling the Forest Service's fire management," and "Personal relationships I have with Forest Service personnel."

However, step-wise multiple regression analyses of the reasons to rely on the Forest Service showed that of the seven reasons listed, only "Procedures that ensure the Forest Service uses effective fire management" was a significant predictor of level of trust (R^2adj. $_{(1, 76)} = 0.13$, $p < 0.001$) and level of SVS (R^2adj. $_{(1, 76)} = 0.12$, $p < 0.001$). Participants who were more trusting of the Forest Service and perceived

Table 5—Correlations between trust, SVS, and reasons to rely on the Forest Service

Reason to rely on the Forest Service	Trust Forest Service		Forest Service shares values	
	r	n	r	n
Past record	0.37**	85	0.34**	84
Laws	0.30	84	0.32**	83
Personal relationships	0.14	84	0.30**	83
Procedures	0.33**	82	0.34**	81
Congress	0.09	81	0.16	80
Opportunity to voice my views	0.21	83	0.15	82
Media	0.31**	83	0.31**	82

**p < 0.01.

greater value similarity agreed that procedures were a good reason to trust, those who were less trusting and perceived less value similarity tended to disagree.

Trust, concern, and knowledge about management—
Individuals with high trust of the Forest Service judged both other residents (r = 0.30, n = 86, $p < 0.01$) and the Forest Service (r = 0.62, n = 86, $p < 0.01$) as having a high level of knowledge of fire management. Trust of the Forest Service was not significantly correlated to one's own level of concern about fire (r = -0.12, n = 86, $p > 0.05$), self-rated knowledge of fire management (r = -0.07, n = 86, $p > 0.05$), or other residents' level of concern (r = -0.13, n = 85, $p > 0.05$).

Trust, fire experiences, and personal consequences—
Participants who had more fire-related experiences such as seeing a fire or knowing someone who lost property were less likely to trust the Forest Service (r = -.0293, $p < 0.01$, n = 83). Likewise, participants who reported more fire-related difficulties such as having waves of strong feelings or feeling watchful and on guard tended to trust the Forest Service less (r = 0.366, $p < 0.01$, n = 80).

Trust, responsibility, and evaluation of prevention effort—
Points assigned to the Forest Service for level of responsibility for fire management were not correlated to level of trust (r = - 0.05, $p > 0.63$, n = 84). Analysis of variance of average trust ratings for grade assigned to effort to prevent fires found a significant main effect ($F_{(4, 76)}$ = 17.85, $p < 0.001$; fig. 5) with those assigning higher grades indicating more trust. Scheffé analysis showed that participants who assigned a grade of A were significantly more trusting of the Forest Service than those assigning any other grade ($p < 0.02$). Those assigning B and C did not differ in trust ($p = 1.0$), nor did those assigning grades of D and F ($p > 0.98$). The B and C graders were more trusting than D and F graders ($p > 0.02$).

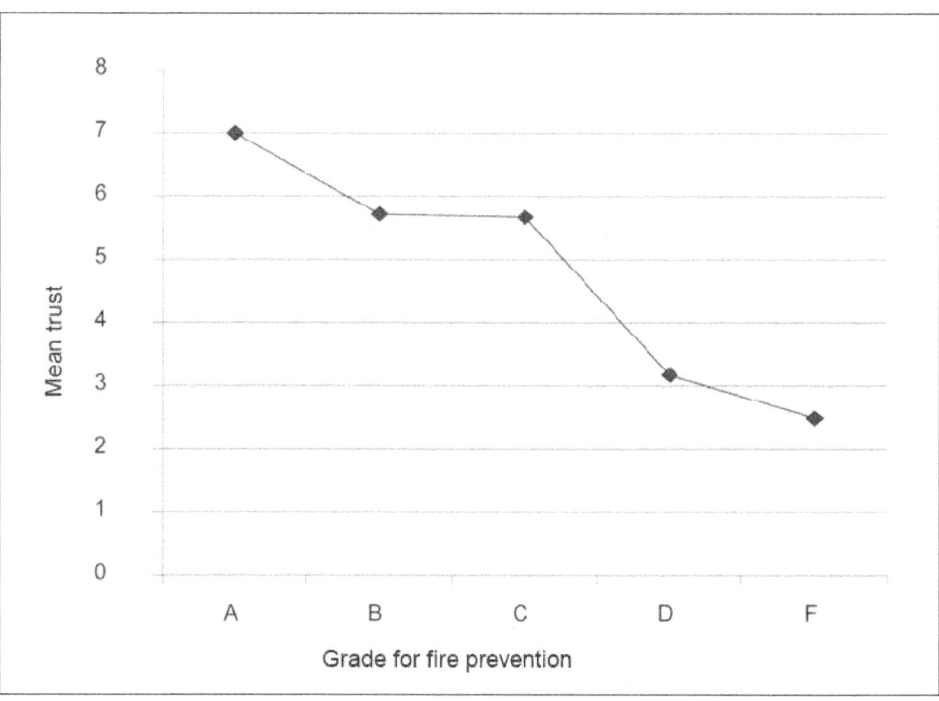

Figure 5—Trust in Forest Service and grade of Forest Service efforts in last year for fire prevention.

Participants who were more trusting of the Forest Service gave higher grades to past efforts and perceived greater value similarity.

A stepwise multiple regression analysis showed that both grade of past fire prevention efforts (R^2adj. $_{(1, 78)}$ = 0.44, $p < 0.001$) and level of SVS (R^2adj. $_{(1, 72)}$ = 0.50, $p < 0.002$) were significant predictors of trust of the Forest Service. Participants who were more trusting of the Forest Service gave higher grades to past efforts and perceived greater value similarity.

Trust, activities, barriers, and communication—
Neither the total number of actions taken to prevent wildfire ($r = -0.06$, n = 81, $p > 0.05$) nor the total number of perceived barriers to personal actions to reduce fire risk ($r = -0.03$, n = 78, $p > 0.05$) were significantly related to trust. Those who trusted the Forest Service less indicated that neighbors ($r = -0.22$, n = 83, $p < 0.05$) and public agencies ($r = -0.28$, n = 82, $p < 0.01$) had not done their part to prevent wildfires and were inclined to report that the Forest Service ($r = -0.25$, n = 79, $p < 0.05$) had not done its part. Preferences for particular sources of information about wildfires and fire management (e.g., local newspapers, e-mail trees, etc.) were not significantly correlated to trust.

Trust, value/action consistency and legitimacy—
We asked participants to indicate how often the Forest Service makes decisions and takes actions consistent with their values, goals, and views. A small portion selected "never" (1.1 percent) or "rarely" (5.6 percent), and about one-fourth (25.8 percent) selected "sometimes." About one-third (33.7 percent) indicated Forest

Service actions were usually consistent with their values, another fourth (24.7 percent) chose "almost always," and a few (2.2 percent) said Forest Service actions were always consistent with their values. Participants were then asked to respond to "If or when the Forest Service makes decisions or takes actions inconsistent with my values, goals, and views, the reasons for doing so are valid." A few disagreed with the statement (3.4 percent completely disagreed, and another 15.7 percent disagreed). Almost one-third (31.5 percent) neither agreed nor disagreed. Almost half agreed that an inconsistency between their own values and Forest Service actions was valid, when it occurred (39.3 percent agreed, 4.5 percent completely agreed). One participant expressed this balance between trust and valid reasons why the agency might not get things done, "I would trust one of them with my life. The only problem is red tape and money constraints." Another participant pointed to policy-related constraints, "What I am thinking is that the people in the Forest Service have the rulebook and are playing by the rulebook and the negligence comes with the change in policy. Maybe we need to have a more flexible policy. I trust the Forest Service people, but they are stuck with the policy and they need to figure a way to change policies."

Participants were categorized as either being above or below the midpoint of the response scales for salient values similarity, value consistency, and legitimacy of inconsistencies. This categorization identified four patterns of responses (table 6).[4]

Figure 6 shows mean trust of groups of participants with each of the patterns of categorical scores. The group of participants who rated salient values similarity low, value consistency low, and legitimacy of inconsistencies low (P1) were the lowest in mean trust ($M = 3.50$, SD $= 2.57$, n $= 10$). The group of participants who rated salient values similarity high, value consistency high, and legitimacy of inconsistencies high (P4) were the highest in mean trust ($M = 6.74$, SD $= 1.12$, n $= 35$). The other two patterns of the three ratings fell between these two extremes in trust of

Table 6—Patterns of ratings of salient values similarity, value consistency, and legitimacy of inconsistencies

Pattern	Salient values similarity Low = 1-4 High = 5-8	Value consistency Low = 1-3 High = 4-6	Legitimacy of inconsistency Low = 1-3 High = 4-5	N
P1	Low	Low	Low	10
P2	High	Low	Low	18
P3	High	High	Low	15
P4	High	High	High	35
Missing				10

---

[4] One individual who was high on SVS, low value consistency, and high on legitimacy of inconsistency was categorized into pattern 2.

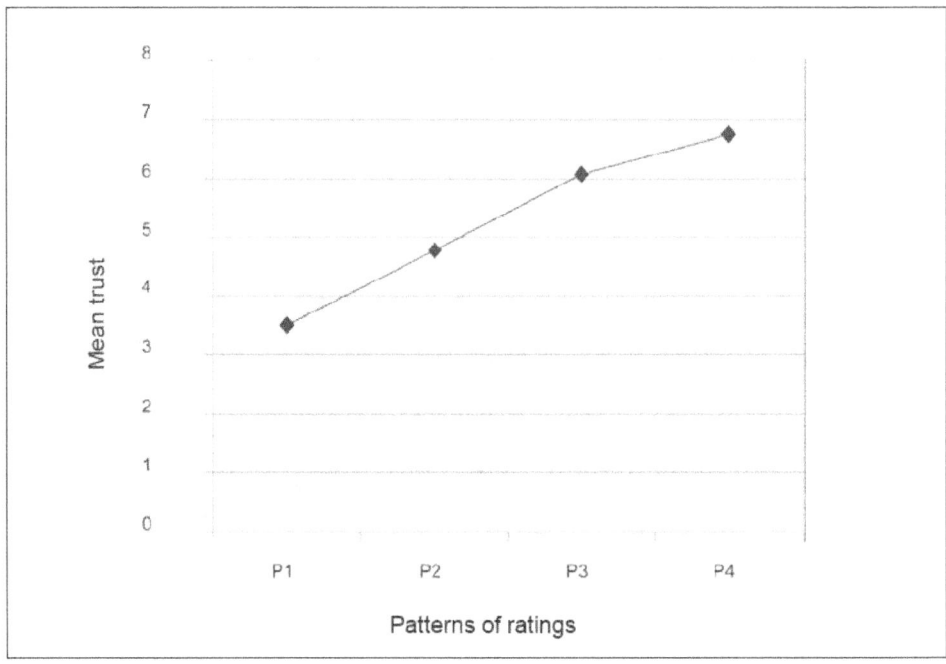

Figure 6—Trust in Forest Service and patterns of salient value similarity (SVS), value consistency, legitimacy of inconsistency (mean trust). P1: low SVS, low value consistency, low legitimacy; P2: high SVS, low value consistency, low legitimacy; P3: high SVS, high value consistency, low legitimacy; P4: high SVS, high value consistency, high legitimacy.

the Forest Service. Analysis of variance of mean trust showed a significant effect for pattern of ratings ($F_{(3, 74)}$ = 21.44, $p < 0.001$). A Scheffé test showed that patterns 1 and 2 were homogeneous and significantly different than the homogeneous subset of patterns 3 and 4 ($p = 0.05$).

Discussion and Conclusion

Experiences in These Fire-Prone Communities

The majority of participants reported multiple fire-related experiences, although a minority had suffered personal injury or personal property loss. Almost half knew others who had suffered loss or damage. Comments about fire risk revealed that many took the risk of fire in stride, as part of living in the mountains. The one exception to this surrounded discussions about prescribed fire, where participants mentioned the risk of fires getting out of control, and the concern surrounding that management technique. A majority indicated that fire had an impact on them directly. The somewhat low rate of reporting stress-related experiences within the last 7 days probably reflected that the last fire event in the study area occurred over a year earlier. Another factor may have been the active role participants have taken in direct actions to reduce fire risk and to educate themselves about fire. This would be an interesting area for further research.

Both personal concern about fires and self-assessed knowledge of fire management were high. As participants lived in fireprone communities and had directly or indirectly experienced fires, these findings are not surprising. This high level of self-assessed knowledge does not seem unreasonable given that self was rated as lower in knowledge than the Forest Service and that other community members were judged to have similar, although somewhat lower, concern and level of knowledge. That almost all of the participants had reported taking personal actions to prevent wildland fires from harming their homes is in line with a high level of self-assessed knowledge. It would be useful for future research to validate both the self-assessed knowledge with an objective measure or test of knowledge about fire and the self-reported fire-risk actions with a direct objective method of assessment.

Responsibility and Performance

Participants were most likely to view agencies, especially the Forest Service, as holding a majority of responsibility for reduction of fire risk, with personal and community responsibility following closely. Agencies, including the Forest Service, personal households, and community were viewed as doing fairly well, although some respondents suggested the Forest Service and neighbors might not have always done their part in reducing fire risk. Although assigned little responsibility overall, tourists and visitors were viewed as doing poorly in reducing fire risk. Comments offered suggest that further limitations on tourists, including more limits on access or more limits on forms of use, were welcomed as additional measures to reduce fire risk.

Spontaneous comments indicated that participants considering the objectives of fire management were thinking about both fire prevention and firefighting. An important identified goal of fire prevention included the establishment and maintenance of healthy forests through various techniques such as fuel removal, reducing tree density, prescribed burns, planning and control of human development, and closure of high-risk areas. Important objectives of firefighting included coordination of different firefighting agencies, effective communication with the public, and making up-to-date information about the status of evacuation routes publicly available. Education was reported as an important objective of fire management by a number of the participants. Participants gave several useful suggestions for education and communication with regard to wildland fire management. Future research might investigate the degree of influence that education has on the actual practice of personal fire prevention activities, including the relative effectiveness of various educational approaches, the fit to differing communities, and the characteristics of those who seek education compared to those who do not.

This demonstrates the importance of following up with community members after meetings and keeping them informed on an ongoing basis.

Implications for Communication and Education

A majority of the participants supported public meetings with the Forest Service, and comments made clear the need to have an open forum where they could ask questions and receive answers from a knowledgeable source. Most of the methods of communication listed are already practiced within these communities to some degree or another, although some expressed the feeling that it had been a while since they had met with the Forest Service and they were starting to feel out of touch with what was going on. Others who did not attend the study sessions expressed a sense of overload on meetings. Clearly a variety of contacts needs to be practiced on an ongoing basis, and the use of community organizations and networks, including the fire safe councils, seems to be an effective vehicle to include. Although media were included in the means of contact, the local paper received more support than television or radio spots. A Web site for current and community-based information seemed to receive strong support. One community declined participation because they were waiting for the agency to act on commitments made in prior meetings. This demonstrates the importance of following up with community members after meetings and keeping them informed on an ongoing basis. Even efforts to meet commitments would probably be helpful to report. If barriers were met, those could also be reported, as it seemed participants understood that funding, policies, and other challenges could prevent the Forest Service from taking action.

Consideration of Future Consequences

Unlike the positive correlations with environment-related attitudes and behavior found by previous research, consideration of future consequences was not found to be strongly related to reactions to and beliefs about wildfires and wildfire management. The few significant correlations found out of the large number calculated could be due to chance. The failure to find significant relationships could be due to the restricted variability of the consideration of future consequences scores for this group of participants. It could also be associated with our limited number of participants; a strong statistical relationship would be needed to detect significance. It is too early to conclude that consideration of future consequences is not related to reported reactions to and beliefs about wildfires and wildfire management. In particular, we expect this measure to have some association with preventative measures that are aimed at reducing risk, especially those that require a more substantial investment of personal resources including time or money.

Trust, Values, Actions, and Risk Responses

Although perceived salient values and trust were significantly related to each other, consistency between perceived shared values and actions taken by the Forest

Service seemed to be more influential in determinations of trust than were the shared values alone. This may have been due to the relatively high average rating of perceived value similarity, paired with low variability. Direct personal experiences with fire, and stressful impacts, were both negatively associated with trust. These results indicate the importance of considering other factors beyond salient values similarity in understanding trust. Those participants who perceived that the Forest Service shared their values but engaged in unjustified value-inconsistent actions reported an average level of trust statistically indistinguishable from participants who perceived that the Forest Service did not share their values.

In line with research regarding other organizations and other risks (Earle and Siegrist 2006), trust was significantly related to perceptions of the Forest Service's past record of effectiveness in reducing fire risk. Given the role of trust in acceptance of agency actions and communications, we expected to find a relationship between direct actions and trust. However, the number of actions taken had no relationship to trust. This has interesting implications for study of the relationship between trust and public response. Only those actions directly advocated through the Forest Service might be expected to be influenced by trust and perceived similar salient values. Reliance on procedures and personal relationships seemed to be a factor in deciding to rely on the Forest Service's fire management efforts. Past record of fire management seemed a bit less important, but was still held by a majority as a reason for reliance.

Trust is the psychological willingness to rely on others or cooperate because of positive expectations of another person's intentions or behavior. Trust is a moral-based evaluation of the character of other people. The correlations with SVS found by this study and other studies indicate that trust is the belief that Forest Service personnel can be relied on because of judged similarity between the citizen's currently active values and the values attributed to the Forest Service. Earle, Siegrist, and colleagues have distinguished confidence as a reason for reliance or cooperation separate from trust (Earle and Siegrist 2006; Earle et al. 2007; Siegrist et. al. 2003, 2005, 2007). Confidence is based on an evaluation of past performance. A perception of good performance leads to a confident feeling that uncertainty is low and that things are under control. Although trust and confidence are appraisals based on different information, the present results indicate that they may be interacting sources of reliance and cooperation. This study's results showed that evaluation of fire prevention efforts during the last year (measured by an assigned letter grade) and level of SVS were both significant predictors of trust of the Forest Service. Participants who were more trusting of the Forest Service both gave higher grades to past efforts and perceived greater value similarity. Also, of seven possible good reasons to rely on the Forest Service, only selection of "past record of fire management" was a significant predictor of both trust and SVS.

A particular kind of past performance, one involving evaluations of moral character, was examined in this study. Consistent with our earlier work (Cvetkovich and Winter 2003), patterns of increasing ratings of SVS, value consistency, and legitimacy of inconsistencies were associated with higher levels of trust.

Taken together, these findings regarding trust and confidence illustrate that forest managers should be aware that judgments of trust are made within a historical context of past performances. Sometimes past performance may be mostly evaluated relative to information that things are under control, as suggested by Earle and Siegrist's (2006) idea of confidence. At other times, past performance may be evaluated relative to moral judgments of shared value similarity, as suggested by the SVS model. It should be noted that for many citizens participating in this study, wildfire management is a high-concern issue. High-concern issues are very likely to invoke moral judgments related to shared values (Cvetkovich and Nakayachi 2007).

Elsewhere we have noted that in addition to information about value similarities and past record, willingness to rely on others and cooperate might be based on other relational assurances (Cvetkovich and Winter 2007). Examples of relational assurances understudied with regard to trust include laws, watchdog activities by nongovernmental agencies and the media, and established personal relationships between citizens and Forest Service personnel. There is a need for future work to investigate how different relational assurances affect trust and confidence.

Gaps and Where We Go From Here

Participants were fairly homogeneous and not representative of the overall populations within these forest communities. Although we made a concentrated effort to recruit seasonal residents, only a few actually participated. A past study sheds light on differences between seasonal and year-round residents of the San Bernardino mountain communities (Vogt and Nelson 2004). Some participants in our study suggested that seasonal residents and those leasing or renting their properties were less concerned, and less similar in values to the Forest Service than were the year-round community members. Additional studies of the perceptions of both seasonal and year-round residents, including how these groups view and are viewed by the Forest Service and other fire management agencies, would be of interest. The lack of relationship between personal actions taken and trust levels was somewhat surprising, although the relatively small sample size and little variance in trust may have suppressed any relationship between these two variables. The interest for meetings with and information from the Forest Service, and an interest in maintaining an ongoing dialogue were made clear. The need to report on actions taken, progress made, and barriers experienced by the Forest Service in its fire management efforts, was affirmed. These steps would assist the agency in continuing to develop trust and a positive basis for interaction in these communities, where individuals sometimes view themselves as very alone in their efforts to reduce risk.

Throughout this study we found that communication approaches have to be varied and tailored to the unique characteristics of what we found to be unique "places" in what might be considered in some views as a predictably homogeneous area. These communities have very distinct connections to the Forest Service. Many community members are active in fire safe councils as well as other community groups and organizations. This diversity of connections affirms the importance of knowing how to fit communication and education efforts to each community, and demonstrates the significant challenge facing the ongoing commitment to reducing fire risk through individual, neighborhood, community, and multiagency engagement.

This diversity of connections affirms the importance of knowing how to fit communication and education efforts to each community, and demonstrates the significant challenge facing the ongoing commitment to reducing fire risk through individual, neighborhood, community, and multiagency engagement.

Acknowledgments

We thank the citizens of the involved communities who made this study possible by giving their time and effort to participate in the study and by helping in other ways. Additional thanks goes to Tricia Abbas, Ruth Wenstrom, Mike Dietrich, Laurie Rosenthal, and Jim Russell, all with the USDA Forest Service, who provided reviews and support in various ways throughout this study. Thanks also to the Inland Empire Fire Safe Council Alliance, especially Laura Dyberg, for their invaluable assistance in helping to arrange sessions and get the word out to members and residents about our study.

Metric Equivalents

1 acre = 0.405 hectare

References

Bonnicksen, T.M. 2003. Written statement for the record. Field hearing on crisis on our national forests: reducing the threat of catastrophic wildfire to central Oregon communities and the surrounding environment. Committee on Resources, U.S. House of Representatives, Redmond, Oregon. August 25, 2003. frwebgate.access.gpo.gov/cgi_bin/getdoc.cgi?dbname_108)house_hearings & docid_f:89089.pdf. p. 24-29. (December 9, 2006).

Collins, C.M.; Chambers, S.M. 2005. Psychological and situational influences on commuter-transport-mode choice. Environment and Behavior. 37(5): 640–661.

Covello, V.T.; Winterfeldt, D.V.; Slovic, P. 1986. Risk communication: a review of the literature. Risk Abstracts. 3(October): 171–182.

Cvetkovich, G.T.; Nakayachi, K. 2007. Trust in a high-concern risk controversy: a comparison of three concepts. Journal of Risk Research. 10(2): 223–237.

Cvetkovich, G.T.; Winter, P.L. 1998. Community reactions to water quality problems in the Colville National Forest: final report. Bellingham, WA: Western Institute for Social Research; Department of Psychology. On file with: Wildland Recreation and Urban Cultures Research Unit, Pacific Southwest Research Station, U.S. Department of Agriculture, Forest Service, 4955 Canyon Crest Drive, Riverside, CA 92507.

Cvetkovich, G.T.; Winter, P.L. 2003. Trust and social representations of the management of threatened and endangered species. Environment & Behavior. 35(2): 286–307.

Cvetkovich G.T.; Winter P.L. 2004. Seeing eye-to-eye on natural resource management: trust, value similarity, and action consistency/justification. In: Tierney, P.T.; Chavez, D.J., tech. coords. Proceedings of the 4th social aspects and recreation research symposium. San Francisco, CA: San Francisco State University: 46–50.

Cvetkovich, G.T.; Winter, P.L. 2007. The what, how, and when of social reliance and cooperative risk management. In: Siegrist, M.; Earle, T.C.; Gutscher, H., eds. Trust in cooperative risk management: uncertainty and skepticism in the public mind. London, United Kingdom: Earthscan: 187–209.

Cvetkovich, G.T.; Winter, P.L.; Earle, T.C. 1995. Everybody is talking about it: public participation in forest management. Paper presented at the American Psychological Association convention. On file with: Wildland Recreation and Urban Cultures Research Unit, Pacific Southwest Research Station, U.S. Department of Agriculture, Forest Service, 4955 Canyon Crest Drive, Riverside, CA 92507.

Earle, T.C.; Siegrist, M. 2006. Morality information, performance information, and the distinction between trust and confidence. Journal of Applied Social Psychology. 36(2): 383–416.

Earle, T.C.; Siegrist, M.; Gutscher, H. 2007. Trust, risk perception and the TCC model of cooperation. In: Siegrist, M.; Earle, T.C.; Gutscher, H., eds. Trust in cooperative risk management: uncertainty and skepticism in the public mind. London, United Kingdom: Earthscan: 1–50.

Ebreo, A.; Vining, J. 2001. How similar are recycling and waste reduction? Future orientation and reasons for reducing waste as predictors of self-reported behavior. Environment and Behavior. 33(3): 424–448.

Freudenberg, W.R.; Rursch, J.A. 1994. The risks of "putting the numbers in context": a cautionary tale. Risk Analysis. 14: 949–958.

Inland Empire Fire Safe Alliance. 2006. Inland Empire communities at risk. http://www.fireinformation.com/IECommunitiesatRisk.html. (December 2, 2006).

Johnson, B.B. 2004. Risk comparisons, conflict, and risk acceptability claims. Risk Analysis. 24: 131–45.

Joireman, J.A. 1999. Additional evidence for validity of the consideration of future consequences scale in an academic setting. Psychological Reports. 84(3, Pt. 2): 1171–1172.

Joireman, J.A.; Van Lange, P.A.M.; Van Vugt, M. 2004. Who cares about the environmental impact of cars? Those with an eye toward the future. Environment and Behavior. 36(2): 187–206.

Joireman, J.A.; Van Lange, P.A.M.; Van Vugt, M.; Wood, A.; Leest, T.V.; Lambert, C. 2001. Structural solutions to social dilemmas: a field study on commuters' willingness to fund improvements in public transit. Journal of Applied Social Psychology. 31(3): 504–526.

Kneeshaw, K.; Vaske, J.J.; Bright, A.D.; Absher, J.D. 2004. Situational influences of acceptable wildland fire management actions. Society and Natural Resources. 17: 477–489.

Langer, G. 2002 (July/August). Trust in government: to do what? Public Perspective: 7–10.

Liljeblad, A.; Borrie, W.T. 2006. Trust in wildland fire and fuel management decisions. International Journal of Wilderness Research. 12(1): 39–43.

Molloy, T. 2004, April 30. Fire threat grows in California forest as trees continue to die. media.www.thebatt.com/media/storage/paper657/news/2004/04/30/News. (December 2, 2006).

Orbell, S.; Perugini, M.; Rakow, T. 2004. Individual differences in sensitivity to health communications: consideration of future consequences. Health Psychology. 23(4): 388–396.

Petrocelli, J.V. 2003. Factor validation of the Consideration of Future Consequences Scale: evidence for a short version. Journal of Social Psychology. 143(4): 405–413.

Rousseau, D.M.; Sitkin, S.B.; Burt, R.S.; Camerer, C. 1998. Not so different after all: a cross discipline view of trust. Academy of Management Review. 23(3): 393–404.

Shindler, B.; Brunson, M.W.; Cheek, K.A. 2004. Social acceptability in forest and range management. In: Manfredo, M.; Vaske, J.; Bruyere, B.; Field, D.; Brown, P., eds. Society and natural resources: a summary of knowledge. Jefferson, MO: Modern Litho Press: 147–158.

Siegrist, M. 2000. The influence of trust and perceptions of risk and benefits on the acceptance of gene technology. Risk Analysis. 20(2): 195–203.

Siegrist, M.; Cvetkovich, G.T.; Roth, C. 2000. Salient value similarity, social trust, and risk/benefit perception. Risk Analysis. 20(3): 353–362.

Siegrist, M.; Earle, T.C.; Gutscher, H. 2003. Test of a trust and confidence model in the applied context of electromagnetic field (EMF) risks. Risk Analysis. 23(4): 705–716.

Siegrist, M.; Earle, T.C.; Gutscher, H. 2005. Perception of risk: the influence of general trust, and general confidence. Journal of Risk Research. 8(2): 145–156.

Siegrist, M.; Gutscher, H.; Keller, C. 2007. Trust and confidence in crisis communication: three case studies. In: Siegrist, M.; Earle, T.C.; Gutscher, H., eds. Trust in cooperative risk management: uncertainty and skepticism in the public mind. London, United Kingdom: Earthscan: 267–286.

Sirois, F.M. 2004. Procrastination and intentions to perform health behaviors: the role of self-efficacy and the consideration of future consequences. Personality and Individual Differences. 37(1): 115–128.

Slovic, P. 2000. Informing and educating the public about risk. In: Slovic, P., ed. The perception of risk. London, United Kingdom: Earthscan Publications: 182–198.

Strathman, A.J.; Gleicher, F.; Boninger, D.S.; Edwards, C.S. 1994. The consideration of future consequences: weighing immediate and distant outcomes of behavior. Journal of Personality and Social Psychology. 66(4): 742–752.

United States Department of Agriculture Inspector General. 2006. Forest Service large fire suppression costs, Report No. 08601-44-SF. http://www.usda.gov/oig/webdocs/08601-44-SF.pdf. (December 8, 2006).

Vogt, C.A.; Nelson, C. 2004. Recreation and fire in the wildland-urban interface: a study of year-round and seasonal homeowners in residential areas nearby three national forests—San Bernardino National Forest, California; Grand Mesa,

Uncompahgre and Gunnison, Colorado; and Apalachicola National Forest, Florida. Michigan State University. Unpublished report. On file with: Wildland Recreation and Urban Cultures Research Unit, Pacific Southwest Research Station, U.S. Department of Agriculture, Forest Service, 4955 Canyon Crest Drive, Riverside, CA 92507.

Weiss, D.S.; Marmar, C.R. 1996. The impact of event scale-revised. In: Wilson, J.; Keane, T.M. eds. Assessing psychological trauma and PTSD. New York, NY: Guilford Press: 399–411.

Winter, G.; Vogt, C.A.; McCaffery, S. 2004. Examining social trust in fuels management strategies. Journal of Forestry. 102(6): 8–15.

Winter, P.L.; Cvetkovich, G.T. 2004a. Is value correspondent action a necessary element of trust? Paper presented at the 84th Western Psychological Association. On file with: Wildland Recreation and Urban Cultures Research Unit, Pacific Southwest Research Station, U.S. Department of Agriculture, Forest Service, 4955 Canyon Crest Drive, Riverside, CA 92507.

Winter, P.L.; Cvetkovich, G.T. 2004b. The voices of trust, distrust, and neutrality: an examination of fire management opinions in three states. Paper presented at the 10th international symposium on society and resource management. On file with: Wildland Recreation and Urban Cultures Research Unit, Pacific Southwest Research Station, U.S. Department of Agriculture, Forest Service, 4955 Canyon Crest Drive, Riverside, CA 92507.

Winter, P.L.; Cvetkovich, G.T. 2007. Diversity in southwesterners' views of Forest Service fire management. In: Kent, B.; Raish, C.; Martin, W., eds. Wildfire risk: human perceptions and management implications. Washington, DC: Resources for the Future Press: 156–170.

Winter, P.L.; Knap, N. 2001. An exploration of recreation and management preferences related to threatened and endangered species: final report for the Angeles, Cleveland, Los Padres and San Bernardino National Forests. Unpublished report. On file with: Wildland Recreation and Urban Cultures Research Unit, Pacific Southwest Research Station, U.S. Department of Agriculture, Forest Service, 4955 Canyon Crest Drive, Riverside, CA 92507.

Winter, P.L.; Palucki, L.J.; Burkhardt, R.L. 1999. Anticipated responses to a fee program: the key is trust. Journal of Leisure Research. 31(3): 207–226.

Appendix A: Fire and Fire Management Questionnaire

Public reporting burden for this information collection is estimated to average 15 minutes per response, with an additional 90 minutes to participate in the group discussion that will follow. This time estimate includes the time required for reviewing instructions, considering responses, completing the form and discussion, and reviewing your completed forms. Send comments regarding this burden estimate or any other aspect of this collection of information, including suggestions for reducing this burden, to Department of Agriculture, Forest Service, 1621 N. Kent Street, Room 800 RPE, Arlington, VA Attention: Clearance Officer; and to the Office of Management and Budget, Paperwork Reduction Project (OMB # 0596-0186), Washington, DC 20503.

The following questions focus on your views about fire and fire management in the San Bernardino National Forest.

Note: For this first set of questions we will ask you about fire management. When we ask about that we are referring to forest management techniques to reduce fire risk as well as fire management and suppression during an actual fire. Please circle one number from 1 to 8 indicating your response to each question. For any item that you are unable or do not wish to answer, circle the "D/K; N/A" ("don't know or no answer") option.

1. How concerned are you about fire and the risk of fire on the San Bernardino National Forest?

0	1	2	3	4	5	6	7	8
D/K N/A	Not at all concerned							Very concerned

2. In your opinion, how concerned are San Bernardino National Forest community residents regarding fire and the risk of fire?

0	1	2	3	4	5	6	7	8
D/K N/A	Not at all concerned							Very concerned

3. How knowledgeable are you about what should be done for effective fire management on the San Bernardino National Forest?

0	1	2	3	4	5	6	7	8
D/K N/A	Not very knowledge-able							Very knowledge-able

4. How knowledgeable do you think San Bernardino forest community residents are about what should be done for effective fire management on the San Bernardino National Forest?

0	1	2	3	4	5	6	7	8
D/K N/A	Not very knowledge-able							Very knowledge-able

5. How knowledgeable do you think the Forest Service is about what should be done for effective fire management on the San Bernardino National Forest?

0	1	2	3	4	5	6	7	8
D/K N/A	Not very knowledge-able							Very knowledge-able

6. To what extent do you believe the USDA Forest Service (FS) *shares your values* about fire management?

0	1	2	3	4	5	6	7	8
D/K N/A	FS does not share my values							FS shares my values

7. To the extent that you understand them, *does the FS have the same goals,* for fire management as you do?

0	1	2	3	4	5	6	7	8
D/K N/A	FS has dissimilar goals							FS has similar goals

8. To what extent does the FS support your views about fire management?

0	1	2	3	4	5	6	7	8
D/K N/A	FS does not support my views							FS supports my views

9. To what extent do you trust the FS in their fire management efforts?

0	1	2	3	4	5	6	7	8
D/K N/A	I completely distrust the FS							I completely trust the FS

10. How often is the following true? "The FS makes decisions and takes actions consistent with my values, goals, and views."

0	1	2	3	4	5	6
D/K N/A	Never	Rarely	Sometimes	Usually	Almost always	Always

11. How much do you agree or disagree with the following? "If or when the FS makes decisions or takes actions inconsistent with my values, goals, and views, the reasons for doing so are valid."

0	1	2	3	4	5
D/K N/A	Completely disagree	Disagree	Neither agree or disagree	Agree	Completely agree

12. There are various reasons why individuals may or may not rely on the Forest Service's fire management on the San Bernardino. Please rate each of the items below, using the following scale:

3 = I strongly agree, this is a reason that I rely on the Forest Service

2 = I agree, this is a reason that I rely on the Forest Service

1 = This is **not** a reason that I rely on the Forest Service

0 = I have no opinion or am not sure

Reasons	Circle one response for each reason			
The Forest Service's past record of fire management	3	2	1	0
The laws controlling the Forest Service's fire management	3	2	1	0
Personal relationships I have with Forest Service personnel	3	2	1	0
Procedures that ensure the Forest Service uses effective fire management	3	2	1	0
Congress holds the Forest Service accountable for its fire management	3	2	1	0
Opportunities that I have to voice my views about fire management	3	2	1	0
Media coverage of Forest Service fire management	3	2	1	0

13. Fire management can accomplish multiple and varied objectives. In your opinion, what are the most important objectives for fire management on this forest?

14. Earlier, we asked about trust of the FS in fire management efforts. In general, do you find people to be:

0	1	2	3	4	5	6	7	8
D/K N/A	Generally not trustworthy							Generally trustworthy

15. Earlier, we asked you about shared values with the FS. We'd also like to know to what extent your fellow community residents share your values about fire management. Would you say that they:

0	1	2	3	4	5	6	7	8
D/K N/A	Do not share my values							Share my values

16. Which of these personal experiences with fire have you had during your lifetime?

Personal Experiences with Fire	Circle no or yes for each	
Saw a wildland fire	No	Yes
Experienced smoke from a wildland fire	No	Yes
A prescribed burn occurred near my home	No	Yes
Experienced road closure due to wildland fire	No	Yes
Was evacuated from my home because of wildland fire or risk of fire	No	Yes
Went without power, shut off to reduce fire risk	No	Yes
Lost or suffered damage to personal property due to a wildland fire *If yes, approximate value of loss -- $*	No	Yes
Family, friend, or close neighbor lost or suffered damage to personal property due to a wildland fire	No	Yes
Was injured by a wildland fire *If yes, please describe*	No	Yes
Family, friend, or neighbor was injured by a wildland fire *If yes, please describe*	No	Yes
Experienced health problems or discomfort caused by smoke from a wildland fire *If yes, please describe*	No	Yes

17. Please rate the degree of impact that fire on the San Bernardino National Forest has had on you directly.

0	1	2	3	4	5	6	7	8
D/K N/A	No impact							Extensive impact

18. Following is a series of questions focused on difficulties people sometimes have after stressful life events. Please indicate which if any of the following difficulties you have experienced during the PAST SEVEN DAYS with respect to the risk of wildland fire.

Difficulties	Circle no or yes for each	
Any reminder brought back feelings about it	No	Yes
I had trouble staying asleep	No	Yes
Other things kept making me think about it	No	Yes
I felt irritable and angry	No	Yes
I avoided letting myself get upset when I thought about it or was reminded of it	No	Yes
I thought about it when I didn't mean to	No	Yes
I felt as if it hadn't happened or wasn't real	No	Yes
I stayed away from reminders about it	No	Yes
Pictures about it popped into my mind	No	Yes
I was jumpy and easily startled	No	Yes
I tried not to think about it	No	Yes
I was aware that I still had a lot of feelings about it, but I didn't deal with them	No	Yes
My feelings about it were kind of numb	No	Yes
I found myself acting or feeling as though I was back at a time when there was a fire	No	Yes
I had trouble falling asleep	No	Yes
I had waves of strong feelings about it	No	Yes
I tried to remove it from my memory	No	Yes
I had trouble concentrating	No	Yes
Reminders of it caused me to have physical reactions, such as sweating, trouble breathing, nausea, or a pounding heart	No	Yes
I had dreams about it	No	Yes
I felt watchful or on guard	No	Yes
I have not experienced any of these difficulties	No	Yes

19. Assuming you have 100 points to characterize full responsibility for reduction of fire risk, please assign the number of points (using whole numbers only please) you think each party has in reducing the risk of wildland fires on the San Bernardino Mountains.

Party	Points
Federal legislators and representatives	
State legislators and representatives	
Scientists and researchers	
Local fire departments	
The U.S.D.A. Forest Service	
California Department of Forestry	
Local business owners	
Visitors and tourists	
My local community	
Me and the people who live with me	
Other (*please fill in*)	
TOTAL	100

20. Taking only those who you assigned points to (even if 1 or 2), please assign each a grade (from A for excellent through F for failing, avoiding pluses or minuses) on how you think they have done in the past 12 months in reducing the risk of wildland fires on the San Bernardino Mountains. If you did not assign points to someone listed, please circle "N/A."

Party		Grade				
Federal legislators and representatives	N/A	A	B	C	D	F
State legislators and representatives	N/A	A	B	C	D	F
Scientists and researchers	N/A	A	B	C	D	F
Local fire departments	N/A	A	B	C	D	F
The U.S.D.A. Forest Service	N/A	A	B	C	D	F
California Department of Forestry	N/A	A	B	C	D	F
Local business owners	N/A	A	B	C	D	F
Visitors and tourists	N/A	A	B	C	D	F
My local community	N/A	A	B	C	D	F
Me and the people who live with me	N/A	A	B	C	D	F
Other (*please fill in*)	N/A	A	B	C	D	F

21. Which of the following actions have you taken as a resident in the San Bernardino Mountains?

Action	Circle no or yes for each action	
Read about home protection from wildland fires	No	Yes
Attended a public meeting about wildland fire	No	Yes
Implemented defensible space around my property	No	Yes
Removed flammable vegetation on my property because I was required to do it	No	Yes
Made inquiries of the local fire department how to reduce risk of property damage from wildland fire	No	Yes
Made inquiries of the local forest ranger how to reduce risk of property damage from wildland fire	No	Yes
Made inquiries of the local Fire Safe Council office or volunteer(s) on how to reduce risk of property damage from wildland fire	No	Yes
Changed structure of my home to reduce risk of property damage from wildland fire	No	Yes
Worked with community effort focused on fire protection	No	Yes
Worked on wildland fire suppression effort as part of paid or volunteer position	No	Yes
Other (*please describe*)	No	Yes

22. If you circled yes for any actions you took that are designed to reduce the risk of losing your home during a wildland fire (in item 21), how effective do you think these actions are?

0	1	2	3	4	5	6	7	8
D/K N/A	Not at all effective							Extremely effective

23. Sometimes there are barriers to effective reduction of fire risk. Among the possible barriers listed below, please circle no or yes to indicate if a barrier (or barriers) apply to reducing the risk of fire in the area immediately surrounding your property.

Barrier	Circle no or yes for each barrier	
I don't have adequate financial resources	No	Yes
My own physical limitations	No	Yes
I don't know who to call/hire to help	No	Yes
I don't want to change the landscape	No	Yes
I don't want to change my roof or other built structures	No	Yes
I am not sure what will really work	No	Yes
I am not worried about fire risk	No	Yes
My neighbors have not done their part	No	Yes
Public agencies have not done their part	No	Yes
The Forest Service has not done its part	No	Yes
Other (*please describe*)	No	Yes

24. For each of the statements below, please indicate whether or not the statement is characteristic of you. If the statement is extremely uncharacteristic of you (not at all like you) please answer "1"; if the statement is extremely characteristic of you (very much like you) please answer "5" next to the question. And, of course, use the numbers in the middle if you fall between the extremes. Please keep the following scale in mind as you rate each of the statements below.

0	1	2	3	4	5
D/K N/A	Extremely uncharacteristic	Somewhat uncharacteristic	Uncertain	Somewhat characteristic	Extremely characteristic

Statement	Circle one answer for each					
I consider how things might be in the future, and try to influence those things with my day to day behavior.	0	1	2	3	4	5
Often I engage in a particular behavior in order to achieve outcomes that may not result for many years.	0	1	2	3	4	5
I only act to satisfy immediate concerns, figuring the future will take care of itself.	0	1	2	3	4	5
My behavior is only influenced by the immediate (i.e., a matter of days or weeks) outcomes of my actions.	0	1	2	3	4	5
My convenience is a big factor in the decisions I make or the actions I take.	0	1	2	3	4	5
I am willing to sacrifice my immediate happiness or well-being in order to achieve future outcomes.	0	1	2	3	4	5
I think it is important to take warnings about negative outcomes seriously even if the negative outcome will not occur for many years.	0	1	2	3	4	5
I think it is more important to perform a behavior with important distant consequences than a behavior with less-important immediate consequences.	0	1	2	3	4	5
I generally ignore warnings about possible future problems because I think the problems will be resolved before they reach crisis level.	0	1	2	3	4	5
I think that sacrificing now is usually unnecessary since future outcomes can be dealt with at a later time.	0	1	2	3	4	5
I only act to satisfy immediate concerns, figuring that I will take care of future problems that may occur at a later date.	0	1	2	3	4	5
Since my day to day work has specific outcomes, it is more important to me than behavior that has distant outcomes.	0	1	2	3	4	5

25. How would you like to receive information from the FS regarding fire and reduction of fire risk?

Source of Information		Your preference	
Articles in our local paper	No	Indifferent	Yes
Attendance at community meetings	No	Indifferent	Yes
Public meetings the FS leads so community can ask questions	No	Indifferent	Yes
Information and displays at FS visitor center	No	Indifferent	Yes
Brochures and pamphlets available on request	No	Indifferent	Yes
Web site	No	Indifferent	Yes
E-mail tree sent by a FS representative and forwarded by Fire Safe Council volunteers	No	Indifferent	Yes
Local television/radio spots, put on by local FS ranger	No	Indifferent	Yes
Other (*please fill in*)	No	Indifferent	Yes

26. Check the highest grade or year of school that you have completed and received credit for.

Highest Grade or Year of School	Check only one
Middle school or less	
High school degree (or G.E.D.)	
At least one year of college, trade, or vocational school	
Graduated college with a Bachelor's degree or equivalent	
At least one year of graduate work beyond a Bachelor's degree or equivalent	
Don't wish to answer	

27. Check the category that contains your age.

Age Group	Check only one
18 to 24	
25 to 34	
35 to 44	
45 to 54	
55 to 64	
65 or over	
Don't wish to answer	

28. Which of the following ethnic groups best describes you?

Ethnic Group	Check
Hispanic or Latino/a	
Not Hispanic or Latino/a	

29. Which of the following racial categories best describes you?

Racial Categories	Check one or more
American Indian or Alaska Native	
Asian	
Black or African American	
Native Hawaiian or Other Pacific Islander	
White, Caucasian, or Euro American	
Another ethnic or racial group	
Don't wish to answer	

30. Check the one category that best describes your household's total income for last year before taxes?

Income	Check only one
Under $5,000	
$5,000 to $9,999	
$10,000 to $14,999	
$15,000 to $24,999	
$25,000 to $34,999	
$35,000 to $49,999	
$50,000 to $74,999	
$75,000 to $99,999	
$100,000 or more	
Don't wish to answer	

31. How many years have you lived in your current home?

Years	

32. How many years have you lived within the perimeter of the San Bernardino National Forest?

Years	

33. What is your ZIP code?

ZIP code	_ _ _ _ _

Appendix B: Focus Group Protocol

Perceptions of Risk, Trust, Responsibility, and Management Preferences Among Fire-Prone Communities on the San Bernardino National Forest

Hello and welcome. I want to thank you for coming here today.

My name is _____ and I am here with _____ and _____.

We will be talking together about the Forest Service, other agencies, and residents in your community regarding fire and fire management. We want your own views as a community member, and will not be expecting you to represent other's opinions or a particular group you belong to aside from yourself. I have a few questions for you, and mostly want to hear from you about what your thoughts are. This is an open discussion and we want to encourage each of you to share your ideas, whether you feel others in the room may have already expressed that idea, or a contradictory opinion to your own. Since we want to hear from each of you, we are asking that you give each other a chance to speak, and that you treat each other with respect. If you have a cell phone with you either turn it to silent mode or turn it off so that our discussion is not interrupted. We will not be attempting to reach consensus on any topic, or ask for any votes.

Your identity will be kept confidential, but we need to identify speakers with their comments, and to match those with the questionnaire. We are using the ID assigned to you and as placed on the notecard in front of you. Once the responses are matched up, your identity is kept separate from the databases we will create. Any contact information we collected to invite you to this meeting will not be stored with these data. If you have any questions or concerns about this please see me at the end of the group session so we can explain our procedures to keep your confidentiality secure.

We will be having our group discussion for the next hour and a half. We will not take any breaks, but if you want to get up and move around feel free to do so quietly. We are tape recording and making written summaries of our discussion. This is just for our use, so we don't miss any of your ideas. These tapes will not be heard by anyone else other than myself and my research coding team. The transcripts will not contain your names. We ask that you speak one at a time, so that the recordings are clear and we can track the discussion.

Most people find these focus group discussions enjoyable and informative. I want to acknowledge that you are of course, under no obligation to answer anything that you do not wish to and that your participation is voluntary so you may leave at any time.

To begin things, let's go around the table and introduce yourselves…some of you may already know each other. Just give your first name, and tell how long you have been a resident of this community. Also, please let us know if this community is your primary or secondary place of residence.

Objectives/Values/Concerns

A. There are numerous objectives that fire management can address on a national forest.

   In your opinion, what objectives for fire management are critical for this forest? Specifically, what should fire management accomplish on this forest…what should it do?

B. What values are linked to the objectives we just discussed?

C. Views on key concerns about fire risk and fire management

   What are your main concerns about fire risk and fire management? Which are most important to you? We are asking you to tell us what concerns you the most about fire, not to evaluate current effectiveness of management. Examples might include scenic beauty, property values, community safety, etc.

D. Now that we've listed your concerns, do we need to go back and revise our objectives? Did we miss something in our first round of objectives that we need to pull in now?

Alternatives

E. What alternative approaches are there for arriving at the objectives this group has listed? Let's try to keep in mind costs, and the desire to address multiple objectives if possible

F. What are the expected impacts and consequences of these various alternatives?

G. What are the risks inherent in each of these alternatives?

H. Which alternatives then, in light of everything we've discussed so far, can you support?

I. What concerns do you have about these alternatives?

J. Now, as we've listed these objectives together, individuals, groups, and agencies were identified. Let's go through these and examine your level of trust in each…What's your level of trust in the various parties you see necessary to address each alternative?

Values/Goals and Trust

K. In the survey we asked you to indicate the level of shared values and goals you hold similar to the FS. What are the most important values and goals that the FS shares with you?

L. What are the most important ones that the FS does not share with you?

M. Thinking back to your trust/distrust rating for the FS, what did you consider in making your rating? Tell me what experiences or information came to mind as you were answering this question. Was it personal interactions, media accounts, or something else?

N. Let's go back to the idea of shared values with the FS, and see if you can think of instances when the FS acted in ways inconsistent with those values. Can you think of examples of when that has happened?

O. And if that happened, were the reasons for inconsistency valid in your mind, that is, when talking about inconsistency, can you think of reasons why that might have occurred? What might be some valid reasons for inconsistency? What might be some instances where inconsistency was not valid?

P. On the questionnaire, we asked the extent to which certain factors, such as the Forest Service's past record on fire management, affect your reliance on their fire management. Other factors were laws, personal relationships, existing procedures, accountability to Congress, opportunities to voice your opinions, and media coverage. What were you thinking about when you answered these questions? Is there anything that has been most influential in your reliance on Forest Service fire management?

Information Needs and Mode of Receipt

Q. What information, if any, would you be interested in receiving or do you feel you need from the FS regarding fires and fire management on this forest?